ROBERT
MORRIS

HOW DO I KNOW?

How Do I Know?
Copyright © 2018 Robert Morris

ISBN: 978-1-945529-03-0

We hope you hear from the Holy Spirit and receive God's richest blessings from this book by Gateway Press. We want to provide the highest quality resources that take the messages, music, and media of Gateway Church to the world. For more information on other resources from Gateway Publishing, go to gatewaypublishing.com.

Gateway Press, an imprint of Gateway Publishing
700 Blessed Way
Southlake, TX 76092
gatewaypublishing.com

 @PsRobertMorris

18 19 20 21 22   5 4 3 2 1
Printed in the United States of America

CONTENTS

NOTE FROM
THE AUTHOR

Imagine for a moment you and I are coworkers. We work in the same office building, and there's a common area where people go to take breaks and eat lunch. One day, I come into the common area, see a chair next to you, and ask if I may sit down. We strike up a conversation and talk about which departments we work in and how long we've been with the company. I say, "You know, I'm very grateful to be back at work. I was out sick for a while. I had an incurable disease that got progressively worse to the point I couldn't walk or talk. I was completely bedridden. My family heard about a new medicine the Food and Drug Administration was testing, and because it wasn't covered by my insurance, they raised the money to cover the cost. The medicine worked, and now I'm totally cured!"

Now, if this had really happened, I'm certain you wouldn't think I was pushing my beliefs on you or trying to shove something down your throat. You wouldn't be offended or angry. On the contrary, you'd be excited for me and happy I no longer had an incurable disease! And it's because I was simply telling you *my story*. I was sharing with you, in an empathetic way, about something that happened to me.

In the same way, I'm not trying to push my beliefs on you through this book. I'm simply telling you my story and sharing the biblical principles and compelling evidence that have shaped my beliefs.

> " I'm simply telling you my story and sharing the biblical principles and compelling evidence that have shaped my beliefs. "

We all have the free will to make our own decisions. I respect your right to believe differently, and I hope as you read this book, you'll give me the same consideration.

In the following pages, I'm going to share *what* I believe and *why* I believe it, and while it may sound strong at times, I urge you to please read to the end. Then, evaluate it. Measure it. Test it. But please give it some thought and consideration because if you do, it can change you from the inside and out.

Robert M—

Robert Morris

INTRODUCTION

I admire people who continuously learn and grow in knowledge. They're not always the most intelligent or formally educated people, but they have a desire to pursue new information and find better ways of doing things. Some do it for self-improvement while others seek advancement in careers that reward higher education or achievement. Still others see it as a way to develop new talents. Whatever the reason, the desire to learn usually begins by asking oneself, "How do I know?"

As we begin our journey with this question, we need to understand the knowledge of God comes to us in two ways: *evidence* and *experience*. The evidence of God is all around us. We see it throughout His creation—the sun, the moon,

> **The knowledge of God comes to us in two ways: *evidence* and *experience*.**

the stars, and all the beauty of God's earth. We also find evidence through studying God's Word as it applies to the world around us. Sometimes we see and evaluate the evidence for ourselves. And other times God does some of the work for us by providing evidence through experience.

The Bible tells us the story of Daniel and his friends, who chose to seek after God instead of earthly temptations. God in turn "gave them knowledge and skill in all literature and wisdom; and Daniel had understanding in all visions and dreams" (Daniel 1:17). These men had direct experience with God because they were open to His revelation. Likewise, the Holy Spirit leads the way for us, "that the God of our Lord Jesus Christ, the Father of glory, may give to you the spirit of wisdom and revelation in the knowledge of Him" (Ephesians 1:17).

Do you have a desire to learn more about the reality of God, the truth of the Bible, and the person of Jesus? Do you have doubts or questions about why you believe what you believe? Are you frustrated with religion? Or do you have a hard time talking to your friends and family about your faith?

Whether you believe in God, still struggle with doubt, or just want to have a better understanding of your faith, this book will help you:

1. **Know there is a God**. There is a supernatural being who created and governs our world and the universe. He is the God of the Bible.
2. **Know the Bible is true**. The Bible is the Word of God and the source of all true knowledge and wisdom, both now and forever.
3. **Know Jesus is the only way**. There is no other name under heaven by which you can be saved. This is a promise for *everyone*.

> **You can trust God to answer your questions and reveal Himself to you if you diligently seek Him.**

The truth is there are mountains of evidence and centuries of miraculous experience to guide us in our search. You can trust God to answer your questions and reveal Himself to you if you diligently seek Him.

I'm excited to share with you how I know *and* how you can know too!

PART ONE

HOW DO I KNOW THERE IS A GOD?

A CORRECT WORLDVIEW

There are some basic questions that help us define our approach to life:

- How did I get here?
- Does my life have a purpose?
- How do I determine right from wrong?
- What happens to me after I die?

We've all asked at least one of these questions, if not all of them, at some point in our lives. They've been discussed at dinner tables and debated in classrooms. While they may seem like deep questions, the answers are the basic principles that shape our values and beliefs and ultimately determine our actions. They make up our *worldview*, which is simply how a person views life and the world around them as a whole.

Any discussions or views we might have about God are greatly affected by our worldview. Many worldviews exist, and in fact, there are many definitions of the word *worldview*.[1] However, Ravi Zacharias, a brilliant theologian who has lectured at major universities around the world, including Harvard, Princeton, Oxford, and Cambridge, explains that we must answer four questions about our *origin, meaning, morality,* and *destiny* to determine a correct worldview. To be fulfilled as a person, these four questions must be answered with consistency and coherency:

1. **Origin:** How did I get here? (Where did I come from?)
2. **Meaning:** Why am I here? (What is the purpose for my life?)
3. **Morality:** How do I define good and evil? (How do I know right from wrong?)

4. **Destiny:** What happens to me after I die? (Is there hope beyond this existence?)[2]

Zacharias believes Christianity is the *only* worldview that provides consistent and coherent answers to these four questions, and I agree. Christianity allows us to live a fulfilling and useful life according to a consistent and coherent worldview.

> 66 **Christianity allows us to live a fulfilling and useful life according to a consistent and coherent worldview.** 99

The Bible doesn't use the word "worldview," but Paul addresses this idea in his warning to believers:

> As you therefore have received Christ Jesus the Lord, so walk in Him, rooted and built up in Him and established in the faith, as you have been taught, abounding in it with thanksgiving. Beware lest anyone cheat you through philosophy and empty deceit, according to the tradition of men, according to the basic

principles of the world, and not according
to Christ (Colossians 2:6–8).

If you're a believer, it's essential for you to
be concerned about your worldview. Not only
will you want to satisfy your own curiosity, but
you'll also want to give true answers to questions
from others about how you live as a Christian.
If you're not a believer, your worldview may be
even more important as it could be the tool that
will guide you to the ultimate truth.

Contrary to popular belief, absolute truth is
not subject to personal opinion in matters such
as origin, meaning, morality, and destiny. Truth
must be understood as that which is founded on
or has its basis in reality. On the other hand,
relativism is a philosophical viewpoint that has
infiltrated the fabric of our society and, sadly,
even the worldview of many believers.
Relativism sees all truth as subjective and argues
there is no objective truth in life. For example, a
relativist might say, "If you believe something
strongly, then it's your truth, but it doesn't make

it my truth." But here is the reality: we can't confuse personal opinion with absolute truth. We can all have differing opinions, but if something is true, it's true regardless of personal opinion. Absolute truth is absolutely true for everyone—no exceptions. The good news is we can

> **Absolute truth is absolutely true for everyone—no exceptions.**

find absolute truth through a biblical Christian worldview. (If you want a more detailed discussion about the Christian worldview, I highly recommend the teachings of Ravi Zacharias.[3])

All other major religions of the world, including Buddhism, Hinduism, and Islam, fail to give adequate answers to at least one of the four questions of origin, meaning, morality, and destiny. John N. Clayton, a former devout atheist, became a Christian in his 20s. He holds multiple advanced degrees with concentrations in physics, chemistry, mathematics, and geology, and he teaches science in public schools. For over 40 years, he has defended the existence of God with his writings and seminars. Clayton describes how he came to accept the Christian worldview rather than those of other religions:

> About this time in my life [in my early 20s], I decided that other religious systems might be as good as the Bible. To check them out, I began reading the Vedas, Koran, Sayings of Buddha, writings of Bahá'u'lláh and Zoroaster, and found that other religions taught many things I could not accept. There were teachings in their writings concerning what life was like after this life that were unrewarding and unrealistic and there were descriptions of God that were illogical and inconsistent. There were also many scientific inaccuracies in their works. There were many teachings about life and how to live it that were not workable. This included the role and position of women in the Koran, the Holy War concept of Mohammed, the pantheism of nearly all other systems, reincarnation, idol worship, polygamy, and a myriad of

ideas which I had expected to find in the Bible, but did not. I began to realize that nothing matched the Bible's system of life. Only in the Bible could I see statements which would stand in the face of the scientific facts that I knew to be true and only the Bible offered a system of life that I felt was reasonable and consistent. I decided that if I ever came to believe in God, it would be a belief based upon the Bible.[4]

Another popular worldview today is evolution, yet it doesn't meet the criteria for being a worldview because it doesn't answer any of the four important questions. It doesn't address *how* we got here or *why* we're here. It essentially says we are just a result of time, matter, and chance.

Our worldview on morality—our understanding of right and wrong—shapes our reactions. Think about this: if we are just matter—physical beings without souls—then why do we have emotions? Why do we react to tragedies? If you saw a person shot and killed, you would react because it would affect your soul (which is made up of your mind, will, and emotions). Evolution does not address this at all. It doesn't address why we're here or our origin. It doesn't address the meaning of life. It doesn't address morality, and it doesn't address destiny. In essence, it says, "You just die, and nothing happens."

Charles Darwin wrote a book in 1859 called *The Origin of Species: By Means of Natural Selection*, and in it, he laid out the theory of evolution. However, it doesn't address the question of origin or original cause. In fact, when Darwin wrote the book, he doubted his own theory so much he devoted two whole chapters to disproving it. He said if evidence didn't come forth in the scientific world in a reasonable amount of time, this theory would be disproved. Over 150 years later, no scientific evidence exists proving that one species mutates into another unique species. Even Darwin admitted the idea of the human eye being formed by natural selection "seems, I freely confess, absurd in the highest possible degree."[5] Most people who believe in evolution haven't even read his book, yet they accept it as truth. I encourage you to study this for yourself. Don't just take my word for it.

Ultimately, we must answer this question: "If life mutated from one simple species to another and another, where did the first living cell come from?" Evolution cannot answer this question of original cause. However, we can find an answer to the origin of life by looking at the matter through a Christian worldview. Finite life can only be created by an infinite source that is capable of doing things our human minds cannot comprehend.[6] The Christian worldview answers the question of origin that an evolutionary worldview cannot.

Likewise, evolution doesn't answer questions of right and wrong, which leads to the popular idea of subjective morality (also known as moral relativism). Those who embrace subjective morality say people should be able to decide what is right or true for them personally. Our culture has even led some believers to think this way.

> **The Christian worldview answers the question of origin that an evolutionary worldview cannot.**

Ravi Zacharias tells the story of a time when one of his college students asked him why he was so afraid of subjective morality—each person deciding what's right for himself or herself. Zacharias responded with a rhetorical question: "Do you lock your doors at night?"[7] His question revealed the student himself was afraid of subjective morality. If morality is subjective, then someone might decide it's moral to put a bullet between his eyes! Because the student instinctively had a concept of right and wrong, he locked his doors at night so someone couldn't enter his home and murder him.

While subjective morality is based on things that change, objective morality is based on things that don't change. Murder is wrong. It isn't *subjectively* wrong; it's *objectively* wrong. Morality must be objective and based on things that don't change. There will always be some things that are right and some things that are wrong.

I've heard people, even Christians, say, "People should be able to decide what's right for themselves." This couldn't be further from the truth! A perfect example of someone who believed in subjective mortality and decided what was right and wrong is Hitler. He didn't see murder as wrong. I've visited Auschwitz twice, and I've seen the heaps of children's eyeglasses left after Hitler had them murdered. I've witnessed the gas chambers where hundreds of thousands of Jews met their death. No one can tell me each person should decide as an individual what is right and what is wrong.[8]

There is a correct worldview. It is consistent and coherent, and it will satisfy your heart and soul. It's the biblical worldview known as *Christianity*.

2

THE FOOLISHNESS
OF ATHEISM

The psalmist David gives us the literal definition of an atheist:

> The fool has said in his heart,
> "*There is* no God" (Psalm 14:1).

Today we might define an atheist as someone who doesn't believe in the existence of God. Yet the definition of an atheist has changed over the years because it is scientifically impossible to justify being an atheist; it is impossible to prove something does *not* exist.

Let me give you an example. If you were to say to me, "There is not a city in Texas called

Paris," I would ask, "Have you been to every city in Texas? Have you done an exhaustive study? Do you have any facts to back up this conclusion?" Well, I happen to *know* there's a Paris, Texas, because I've *been* there. I grew up in East Texas—which, I might add, is nothing like Paris, France—and Paris *is* in East Texas. It's a small town, and their landmark is a small-scale replica of the Eiffel Tower with a cowboy hat on top. The comparisons end there, but it does exist, and I can prove it because I have firsthand knowledge of it.

To prove something does *not* exist, to prove there is no God, you would have to be omniscient—to have all knowledge. The problem is no one has all knowledge. No one knows everything! There are some very intelligent people in this world, but how many of them know all languages

> **" To prove something does *not* exist, to prove there is no God, you would have to be omniscient—to have all knowledge. "**

and can speak them fluently? Who can diagram every sentence in every language? Who knows everything about mathematics, including algebra, geometry, trigonometry, and calculus? Who knows the history of every culture and every nation? What contestant has ever answered every question correctly on the game show Jeopardy? Of course, none of these people exist!

Think about it this way: how much does the smartest person in the world know? Is it possible the smartest person in the world has one percent of all knowledge? Suppose this person even has two percent of all knowledge. Then is it possible the smartest person in the world knows everything? Absolutely not!

Many well-known scientists have believed in God. Lord Kelvin said, "If you study science deep enough and long enough, it will force you to believe in God." He also said, "The atheistic idea is so nonsensical that I do not see how I can put it in words."[1]

These are the reasons the Bible says atheism is foolish. A foolish person says something does not exist even though he doesn't have all knowledge. What he should say is, "I don't know *if* there is a God," which would make him an agnostic. Gnostic comes from the Greek word *gnosis*, which means knowledge. A– is a single-letter prefix that means "not." An agnostic is someone who says he does not know something. If he is speaking about God, he is saying he doesn't know if there is a God. The word "atheist" is also based on the Greek word *theos*, which means God. Add the same prefix, and an atheist is a person who says there is no God. Atheists and agnostics may have some similar ideas, but an atheist rejects the idea of God outright, whereas an agnostic is open to the possibility of God, given further evidence.[2] So what are some of the further arguments (or evidences) for God's existence?

A few years ago, while my wife, Debbie, and I were on vacation, we had a cabana at the hotel pool next to a young couple from India. We started talking with them, and before long, we were engaged in a good conversation. When the waiter brought the menu over to us at dinnertime, they asked us what was good to eat, and we gave them some recommendations. The wife asked if we thought they could order particular menu items without meat. We said we thought they could, and I asked her if she was a vegetarian. She said she was, so I followed up by asking, "Are you a vegetarian for dietary or religious reasons?"

"Religious reasons," she responded.

"Are you a Hindu?" I asked.

She replied, "Yes." Then, pointing to her husband, she said, "But he's an atheist." Her husband interjected, "Well, I used to say I am an atheist but not anymore. Now I say I'm an agnostic."

Having told them I was a pastor earlier in our conversation, I said, "Well, it's interesting to hear you say that because I'm about to share something related to this with our church. May I share it with you and see if it would be offensive to you?"

He said I could, so I said: "I don't believe it's scientifically possible to be an atheist. I don't think anyone can say for sure that something *doesn't* exist when no one can know everything. But I think someone can say, 'I don't know if something exists.'"

"It's not offensive to me at all," he said. "Actually, it's why I've changed. I cannot positively say there is no God. I don't think I have the ability to say that, so now I say I don't know *if* there is a God."

Even a formerly self-proclaimed atheist can't say God doesn't exist!

3

I KNOW HIM PERSONALLY

You might turn my earlier reasoning around on me and ask, "If I don't have all knowledge and can't say definitively there is *no* God, how can you say definitively there *is* a God, Pastor Robert?" The reason I can say I know there is a God is because I know Him personally.

Take my example about saying there is no such place as Paris, Texas. Now, change the city to a person. Suppose you said to me, "There is no Tom Lane." Then I would ask you this question: "Have you met every single person in the world?" Of course, you haven't! You can't tell me there is no Tom Lane if you haven't met every person in the world. However, I don't have to meet every person in the world to know there is a Tom Lane. Instead, I only need to have met Tom Lane. And I can tell you definitively there *is* a Tom Lane because I have met him, I talk with him, and he is my friend. I have a personal relationship with Tom Lane.

In the same way, I can tell you there is a God because I have met Him, I talk with Him, and He is my friend. I have a personal relationship with God. So do millions of other believers throughout the world. And so can you!

> **I can tell you there is a God because I have met Him, I talk with Him, and He is my friend. I have a personal relationship with God.**

This Is How I Know There Is a God:

1. I know there is a God because the Christian worldview is the *only* one that satisfactorily answers the key questions

about humanity's origin, meaning, morality, and destiny.

2. I know there is a God because atheism, the denial of God's existence, is foolishness and a scientific impossibility.

3. I know there is a God because I, and millions of others throughout the world, have met Him, talked with Him, and become His friend. I have a personal relationship with Him.

FOR DISCUSSION & PERSONAL REFLECTION

Focus

We should know why we believe God exists, and a correct worldview helps us understand what we believe. Christians can say they absolutely know there is a God because they have met Him, talked with Him, and become His friend. They have a personal relationship with Him.

Key Scripture

The fool has said in his heart,
"*There is* no God" (Psalm 14:1).

Review

There Is a Correct Worldview

A worldview must satisfactorily answer these four questions to be considered a correct worldview:

1. **Origin:** How did I get here? (Where did I come from?)
2. **Meaning:** Why am I here? (What is the purpose for my life?)
3. **Morality:** How do I define good and evil? (How do I know right from wrong?)
4. **Destiny:** What happens to me after I die? (Is there hope beyond this existence?)

Christianity answers all four.

Two examples of an incorrect worldview are evolution and subjective morality. Evolution doesn't answer the question of origin. It says one species mutates into another, but no species has accomplished this before or since Charles Darwin wrote his book on evolution. In addition, this theory cannot explain the creation of the first species. Subjective morality means each person decides what is right for him, and there is no absolute right or wrong. This philosophy creates chaos and destruction.

Atheism is Foolishness

An atheist is a person who says, "There is no God." In order to make this statement, a person must have all knowledge; he must know everything. The smartest person in the world would have less than one percent of all knowledge, but even if this person had two percent of all knowledge, he would have to admit God might exist within the remaining 98% of knowledge he does not have. It's impossible to claim something doesn't exist if you don't know everything. An agnostic is a person who says, "I don't know if there is a God." Psalm 14:1 states it's foolish to say there is no God.

There Is a God, and I Know Him

Even without all knowledge, you can say something or someone exists. If you have met a person, you know this person exists, especially if you have talked to each other and are friends. We can say the same truth about God. When you know Him, you are forever changed. He created you with a mind to think, a heart to feel, and a will to choose. He wants us to choose to love, serve, and follow Him. He wants to talk to us and be our friend.

Discussion or Personal Reflection

1. Has your worldview changed after reading this section? How will a correct worldview affect your interactions with people who don't believe?

2. Subjective morality is the philosophy that says each person decides what is right individually. What are the flaws in

this worldview? Can you think of some examples of subjective morality in today's society?

3. Briefly describe how Christianity answers each of the four questions that qualify it as a correct worldview.

- **Origin:** How did I get here? (Where did I come from?)
- **Meaning:** Why am I here? (What is the purpose for my life?)
- **Morality:** How do I define good and evil? (How do I know right from wrong?)
- **Destiny:** What happens to me after I die? (Is there hope beyond this existence?)

4. How could you respond to an agnostic who challenges the existence of God and your faith in Him? In addition, what are some ways you can speak the truth in love if they speak down to you?

5. How do you personally know God exists?

6. Write about how you know God exists and how He's changed your life. Read through your notes over the next week and ask the Lord to give you the opportunity to share your story with someone else.

Take It with You

- It's important to know your own worldview.
- There must be an absolute right and wrong.
- Evolution is an unproven theory and not a valid worldview.
- Use the four points of a worldview as a basis to discuss your faith with others.
- Your relationship and experience with God as Lord of your life will be evidence to others He exists.

Prayer

Almighty God, I adore You and acknowledge You as the one true God, Creator of heaven and earth. Thank You for giving me Your Son, Jesus, as a sacrifice for my salvation. Thank You, Lord, for Your Word and the Holy Spirit to guide me. Show me the people in my life who need to know You and give me the courage to speak Your truth in love. In Jesus' name, Amen.

PART TWO

HOW DO I KNOW THE BIBLE IS TRUE?

4

THE BIBLE IS AMAZING

Have you ever thought about how accurate and consistent the Bible is? What's written within our modern Bible is miraculously identical to the oldest known ancient manuscripts. The Bible is also internally consistent with itself and externally congruent with history. It's truly amazing!

When examining any ancient document, three manuscript tests are used to determine the reliability of what is written. These three tests are known as the bibliographic test, the internal evidence test, and the external evidence test.

The bibliographic test determines the accuracy of the Bible as it was recorded throughout history. It tests to see if our current Bible includes the original words and content. If the centuries either diluted or perverted the content, then the reliability of the Bible would be in question. The bibliographic test first examines the number of ancient Bible documents in existence for comparison to our current Bible. The Bible has no equal when it comes to the number of ancient manuscripts; the New Testament alone boasts over 25,000! The average number of surviving manuscripts for any single book from the ancient world is about 10 to 20. The closest rival in number is Homer's *Iliad*, but even this has only 643 ancient manuscripts in existence. In the realm of ancient documents, the New Testament has a massive cache of evidence, and the consistency of the documents confirms its validity.

The gap between the writing of the New Testament and existing fragments is also an astonishing 25 years. The average gap between any other ancient writing and its first copy is about 1,000 years. While scholars continue to question the reliability of the New Testament, few would question the reliability of Homer's *Iliad* even though there's far less evidence to support it.[1]

Bruce Metzger was a renowned Bible scholar and textual critic who served as a professor at Princeton Theological Seminary. He is considered one of the most influential Bible scholars of modern times and is credited with chairing one of the most exhaustive examinations of the Bible text in history. He found that even with centuries of transcription, the Bible maintains its accuracy and consistency. In fact, when Metzger tested these factors, he found remarkable accuracy in the thousands of New Testament manuscripts compared to the handful of other ancient documents. When compared to Homer's *Iliad* or the ancient Hindu *Mahabharata*, the New Testament stands alone. Metzger also conducted a study showing the current copies of the *Mahabharata* represent only about 90% of the original document while Homer's *Iliad* contains about 95%.[2] Five to ten percent corruption between small numbers of manuscripts is a massive discrepancy. The New

Testament manuscripts, however, produced a different result. In the same studies, Metzger found the New Testament manuscripts to be 99.5% accurate and consistent across thousands of ancient manuscripts. The 0.5% Metzger discovered were only grammatical errors rather than content errors.

This again puts the New Testament in an elite class all by itself. If any one of the writers of the Gospels or the book of Acts had embellished, then we would have contradictions in persons, places, dates, and events. And if any of the transcribers throughout history had chosen to construct stories and/or fabricate events, then massive contradictions would exist in the ancient manuscripts. But they don't. The massive contradictions are simply *not* there. The bibliographic evidence for the reliability of the Bible is unarguably sound. The bottom line is this:

❝ The bottom line is this: what was written thousands of years ago is what we read in our Bibles today. ❞

what was written thousands of years ago is what we read in our Bibles today.

While the bibliographic test determines if the current Bible is the same as the original texts, the internal evidence test determines the accuracy of those texts. Think about the writings of other faiths. Writings about Buddha are the sermons of one man. The Qur'an contains the words of one man compiled by others after he died. The Bible, on the other hand, consists of 66 books by 40 different writers over a period of 1,500 years (from the 14th century BC until about 100 AD). Very few writers of the Bible ever met, and collusion over 1,500 years would be impossible. However, the internal evidence proves to be miraculously consistent.

Seven hundred years before Jesus' arrival, Isaiah wrote about His virgin birth, and Micah named Bethlehem as the city where He would be born. King David wrote about Jesus' crucifixion 1,000 years before He was nailed to a cross and 500 years before any historical record of the practice of crucifixion. In fact, the first recorded crucifixion was in the fifth century BC.

Another remarkable writing in the Bible is by the prophet Daniel, who wrote around 500 BC. He prophesied about a great empire that would dominate the world and then suddenly be cut off. Daniel wrote it would later be divided into four empires, and those four empires would become two. Those two would become one, and then the Messiah would come. Please understand Daniel wrote about all these details 500 years before Jesus was born—and every one of them came true. This is incredible internal evidence for the reliability of the Bible.

The external evidence test examines other historical documents written during the same time as the Bible to determine if a text is confirmed or contradicted by external documents. External evidence is also found in archeology and geography.

Around 300 BC, Alexander the Great came to power. He dominated most of the known world until he was killed—at age 32. His kingdom was divided among his four generals and became four empires. Those four became two, the Seleucid and Ptolemaic empires. And eventually, those empires merged to become one—the Roman Empire. What an amazing series of events Daniel predicted centuries before they happened! The accuracy of Daniel's writings rightly confounds historians. It's just one example of the undeniable external historical evidence found in the Bible.

People often ask me, "How do you know the Bible is true?" I respond by turning this question around and asking, "How do you know it's *not* true?" Surely it would be easy to prove the Bible is *not* true. You could find a city the Bible speaks about that never existed. You might look for instances

> 66 **People often ask me, 'How do you know the Bible is true?' I respond by turning this question around and asking, 'How do you know it's *not* true?'** 99

where the Bible references cities 100 miles apart that were actually 200 miles apart. It should be very easy to contradict, but *no one* can do it. Bruce Metzger made this statement: "After you take the 20,000 lines of the New Testament, it is safe for any scholar to say 99.5% of the Bible has been corroborated by other historical documents."[3]

The Bible is amazingly and miraculously accurate, and the bibliographic, internal, and external evidence solidifies its reliability. It is remarkable how many other historical documents confirm what is written in the Bible.

Christ came 2,000 years ago, and nearly 3,500 years have passed since the first Scriptures were written. No book has been more thoroughly studied. No text has been more painstakingly scrutinized. Yet it has always been proven true. The mathematical odds are ridiculous that 40 writers could produce 66 books over a span of 1,500 years that are so congruent. It would be impossible if it was not true!

The work of Dr. Peter Stoner, the late professor emeritus of science at Westmont College, provides another example of the extraordinary congruence of the Bible. In the 1950s, Dr. Stoner commissioned a study of Bible prophecy. The goal was to consider the mathematical probability of Messianic prophecies being fulfilled. He based this research strictly on historical documentation of events of the time and did not use the Bible to validate itself. The question was, "What is the chance that any man might have lived from the day of these prophecies down to the present time and have fulfilled all of the eight prophecies?"[4]

About 600 students from 12 classes in Christian Evidences at Westmont College were involved in this process. They looked at individual prophecies and determined what the mathematical odds were that they could take place. Initially, as an example, they looked at the odds that the Messiah would be born in Bethlehem (Micah 5:2). Just taking the population of the world at that time and dividing it by the population of Bethlehem, they determined the odds of Jesus being born in Bethlehem were one in 300,000! (In fact, such an estimate was conservative since they didn't take into account other limiting factors, such as Jesus did not live in Bethlehem. He was there only due to the edict of the Roman census at the precise time Mary was ready to deliver.)

There are over 50 Messianic prophecies with over 300 references in the Bible. The Westmont group decided the task of calculating all of them would be overwhelming (and, as you will see, unnecessary). Instead, they chose eight well-known prophecies and calculated the probabilities of their fulfillment.

The students calculated each probability based on assumptions they agreed upon and then reviewed and revised them to be especially conservative. Since each prophecy was independent of the others, they multiplied the result of each calculation by the next. Based on those eight prophecies alone, the group calculated the probability that all of them could be fulfilled by one person to be one in 10 to the 17th power (10^{17}). That's one in 100,000,000,000,000,000. One in 100 quadrillion! What an extraordinary "coincidence" that would make!

Dr. Stoner submitted his figures to a committee of the American Scientific Affiliation for review. After examining the methodology, the affiliation verified his calculations were dependable and accurate in regard to the scientific material presented.[5]

Clearly, this number may be difficult for some to comprehend, so Dr. Stoner offered a way to visualize the odds:

> If you mark one of ten tickets, place all of the tickets in a hat, thoroughly stir them, and then ask a blindfolded man to draw one, his chance of getting the right ticket is one in ten. Suppose we take 10^{17} silver dollars and lay them on the face of Texas. They will cover all of the state two feet

❝Scripture is inspired by God.❞

deep. Now mark one of these silver dollars and stir the whole mass thoroughly, all over the state. Blindfold a man and tell him he can travel as far as he wishes, but he must pick up one silver dollar and say it's the right one. What chance would he have of getting the right one? Just the same chance the prophets would have had of writing these eight prophecies and having them all come true in any one man, from their day to the present time, providing they wrote using their own wisdom.[6]

Jesus fulfilled them all!

5

THE BIBLE SAYS SO

I f you grew up in a Christian home, you probably sang the lyrics, "Jesus loves me! This I know, for the Bible tells me so...." The truth is we can *know* because the Bible says so! And the overwhelming evidence proving the miraculous reliability of the Bible makes it truly amazing! This means if you're a believer, you can *know* the Scriptures support your belief in God's Word.

If you're a Christian, you'll find it's good to know the Bible provides substantial evidence for its authenticity. Jesus quoted from about three-fourths of the Old Testament books, and He always called them "Scripture." When Satan tempted Jesus, the Bible records Jesus saying three times, "It is written ... It is written ... It is written" (Matthew 4:4, 7, 10). In fact, Jesus defeated Satan by presenting him with the truth in the Scriptures! Jesus believed the writings of the Bible were authentic and "God-breathed." He knew, as it is written, that Scripture is inspired *by* God. Men wrote it, but the Holy Spirit inspired their words. The apostle Paul says:

> All Scripture *is* given by inspiration of God, and *is* profitable for doctrine, for reproof, for correction, for instruction in righteousness (2 Timothy 3:16).

The phrase "given by inspiration" is just one word in Greek: *theopneustos*. It comes from the words *theos* (God) and *pneuma* (breathe or breath). Bible translators have also rendered this verse as "All Scripture is God-breathed." Think about it this way: when you're speaking, you're breathing out. This is why when you speak, you have to stop occasionally and take a breath. In the same way, God spoke—breathed—the Bible to men, and they wrote what they were inspired by God to write. Consider what the apostle Peter says:

> **"Jesus is the truth, so it's important for His Word, the Bible, to be written."**

> Knowing this first, that no prophecy of Scripture is of any private interpretation, for prophecy never came by the will of man, but holy men of God spoke *as they were* moved by the Holy Spirit (2 Peter 1:20–21).

So why is it important for the Scriptures to be written? If you were to enter into a contract, most likely you would prefer for it to be in writing rather than a simple verbal agreement. You might even use the phrase, "Will you put that in writing?" You can't trust it to be true if it's not in writing because it can change.

I heard a story once about a doctoral student who was doing his dissertation. He disagreed with the dissertation process, so he decided to make a point during his dissertation by making profound statements and attributing them to people he knew. For example, he would say, "As told to me by Johnny the waiter at Denny's." Then he would make another statement and say, "As told to me by the bellman at the Holiday Inn." After a little while his professor stopped him and said, "You can't do this in a dissertation. You must have written documentation with footnotes to prove what you're saying is true. You can't say 'as told to me by the waiter.'" Perplexed, the student asked, "Why does it have to be written? Why is it more important if it's written than if it's verbal?" The professor thought for a moment and said, "Okay, I see where you're going. Proceed." So the student continued his dissertation. A few months later the professor contacted him and said, "I want you to know we passed you. You'll be receiving your Ph.D., but we're not giving it to you in writing. You'll just have to take our word for it."

If it's true, it needs to be written. John 14:6 says Jesus is "the way, *the truth*, and the life" (emphasis added). Jesus is the truth, so it's important for His Word, the Bible, to be written.

6

I KNOW THE AUTHOR PERSONALLY

A few years ago, a pastor was getting ready to introduce me at a conference. Before he walked up to the platform, he leaned over and said, "You know Robert, as I was looking at how many of your books have made the bestseller list, I was wondering how you want me to introduce you." I responded, "Just tell them I know the author of the bestselling book of all time, and He's a personal friend of mine!"

The bestselling book of all time is the Bible, God is the author, and I know him personally! And if you've met Jesus, you know Him too!

As I've explained, we can know the Bible is true from scientific and logical reasoning. The consistent evidence in the Bible points to a

person. It points to the infinite original cause.
It points to the Bible's one author—God! And
like me, millions of people throughout the
world know the author—not just because of the
evidence but through *experience*. We know the
author personally as all the evidence converges
in one person—Jesus Christ. All it takes to get
to this next level is a step of faith. Not a leap of
faith but just a small step to connect with Jesus.

Here's what the Bible says about it:

> "You search the Scriptures because you
> think they give you eternal life. But the
> Scriptures point to me!" (John 5:39 NLT).

> In the beginning was the Word, and the
> Word was with God, and the Word was
> God (John 1:1).

> And the Word became flesh and dwelt
> among us (John 1:14).

We know the Bible is true because Jesus
became flesh and lived on this earth. We have

evidence of His life, and it's documented He was crucified and rose on the third day. When He rose from death, appeared to 500 of His

> **We know the Bible is true because Jesus became flesh and lived on this earth.**

disciples, and gave the Holy Spirit at Pentecost less than two months later, Jesus enabled all who have faith in Him to *experience* His presence.

If you still wonder if the Bible is true and if Jesus is who He says He is, take a moment and answer these questions:

- How did He arrange to be born into a specific family?

  "When your days are fulfilled and you rest with your fathers, I will set up your seed after you, who will come from your body, and I will establish his kingdom. He shall build a house for My name, and I will establish the throne of his kingdom forever" (2 Samuel 7:12–13).

- How did He arrange to be born in a specific city, in which His parents didn't live?

> "But you, Bethlehem Ephrathah,
>   *Though* you are little among the thousands
>   of Judah,
>   *Yet* out of you shall come forth to Me
>   The One to be Ruler in Israel,
>   Whose goings forth *are* from of old,
>   From everlasting" (Micah 5:2).

- How did He arrange His own death, and specifically by crucifixion, with two others?

> Therefore I will divide Him a portion
>   with the great,
>   And He shall divide the spoil with the
>   strong,
>   Because He poured out His soul unto
>   death,
>   And He was numbered with the
>   transgressors,
>   And He bore the sin of many,

And made intercession for the
    transgressors (Isaiah 53:12).

- How did He arrange to have His executioners gamble for His clothing?

They divide My garments among them,
And for My clothing they cast lots
    (Psalm 22:18).

- How did He arrange to be betrayed in
  advance and to be crucified on the exact
  day?

Then I said to them, "If it is agreeable
to you, give *me* my wages; and if not,
refrain." So they weighed out for my
wages thirty *pieces* of silver.
And the Lord said to me, "Throw it to
the potter"—that princely price they set on
me. So I took the thirty *pieces* of silver and
threw them into the house of the Lord for
the potter (Zechariah 11:12–13).

- How did He arrange to have the executioners carry out the regular practice of breaking the legs of the two victims on each side but not His own?

  He guards all his bones;
  Not one of them is broken (Psalm 34:20).

- How did He arrange to come back to life on the exact day He said He would?

  From that time Jesus began to show
  to His disciples that He must go to
  Jerusalem, and suffer many things from
  the elders and chief priests and scribes,
  and be killed, and be raised the third day
  (Matthew 16:21).

This Is How I Know the Bible Is True:

1. The Bible is 66 books written by 40 different writers over a period of 1,500 years. The written Word is proven to be

bibliographically, internally, and externally reliable. I know the Bible is true because the Bible confirms itself.

2. The Bible is an amazing book! It is congruent with truth beyond all reasonable probability. We can know the Bible is true because of the evidence.

3. The Bible's story converges in one person—Jesus Christ. You can know the Bible is true because you can *experience* Jesus.

FOR DISCUSSION & PERSONAL REFLECTION

Focus

The 66 books of the Bible were written over a period of 1,500 years by 40 different writers. They are consistent with history, congruent with truth, and converge in one person, Jesus Christ, God's Son.

Key Scriptures

All Scripture *is* given by inspiration of God, and *is* profitable for doctrine, for reproof, for correction, for instruction in righteousness (2 Timothy 3:16).

> Knowing this first, that no prophecy of
> Scripture is of any private interpreta-
> tion, for prophecy never came by the
> will of man, but holy men of God spoke
> *as they were* moved by the Holy Spirit
> (2 Peter 1:20–21).

Review

The Bible Says So

If you're a Christian, you'll find it's good to know the Bible provides substantial evidence for its authenticity. Jesus refers to over three-fourths of the Old Testament's books as "Scripture." Scripture is "God breathed." Men wrote it, but the Holy Spirit inspired their words.

The Bible Is Amazing

The fact that all 66 books are congruent in content when 40 men wrote them over a span of 1,500 years is truly amazing! There are over 50 Messianic prophecies with over 300 references in the Bible. There is a 1 in 10^{17} chance that all eight of the historically proven prophecies we mentioned could happen by chance. Those odds are beyond human comprehension. Only God has the power to make something like this happen.

I Know the Author Personally

The entire Bible points to Jesus, and we must choose to step out and believe in Him. He fulfilled every prophecy in the Old Testament, which was written hundreds of years earlier. Jesus, the Word, became flesh and lived on this earth. His death and resurrection have been historically documented. He endured and conquered death for our salvation.

Discussion or Personal Reflection

1. What is your favorite story in the Bible? What do you like about it?
2. Think of a time when you needed direction, encouragement, or wisdom and you found it in the Bible. What was the situation, and how did God's Word speak to you?

3. What is your basis for believing the Bible is true?

4. What would you say to someone who challenged the historical accuracy of the Bible?

5. How would you share that you know the author of the Bible?

Take It with You

- The Word of God has stood the test of time.
- Jesus referenced the Old Testament as "Scripture."
- Jesus' birth, death, and resurrection are historically documented.
- The odds of biblical prophecies occurring by chance are astronomically small. Only God could make them happen with complete accuracy in the way the Bible records them.
- The Bible points to a person, Jesus Christ.
- For more information or evidence on the authenticity of the Bible, visit Ravi

Zacharias' website (rzim.org) or read the
book *The New Evidence That Demands a
Verdict* by Josh McDowell.[1]

Prayer

Lord God, thank You for Your Word. Thank
You for revealing the intricate details of Your
plan through the prophecies of the Bible. Thank
You for the evidence that Your Word is true.
Help me to spend time in Your Word and to
meditate on it even more. Thank You for Your
Son, Jesus, who is the Word made flesh. All
glory and honor are Yours, Lord. In Jesus' name,
Amen.

PART THREE

HOW DO I KNOW JESUS IS THE ONLY WAY?

7

GOD IS GOOD

C hristianity is not exclusive, but the Bible is clear there is only one way to become a Christian, and it's through Jesus Christ. Yet many people take exception to the statement "Jesus is the *only* way." Unbelievers see it as a difficult concept because it seems so exclusive. Even some believers struggle with it as they wonder about non-Christians who are sincerely seeking God. However, two Scriptures plainly show us Jesus is the only way:

> Jesus said to him, "I am the way, the truth, and the life. No one comes to the Father except through Me" (John 14:6).

"There is no other name under heaven given among men by which we must be saved" (Acts 4:12).

Notice, in John's gospel, Jesus does not say He is *a way* or *one of the ways*; He says He is the *only way*. Likewise, in Acts, His is the *only name* by which salvation can take place. Many people reject Christianity because they think these passages make it too exclusive.

Of course, the reality is all religions are exclusive. Buddhism, Hinduism, Islam, and other religions require belief in certain ideals and principles, as well as following certain codes and rules, to achieve or earn whatever eternal promise these religions offer. Some religions or belief systems offer nothing of value beyond this mortal life. Even atheism is exclusive since you must *not* believe in God to be an atheist.

The Christian faith, on the other hand, is actually the most inclusive of any religion in the world, although I don't like to call it a "religion". Religion is a human's attempt to get to

God; Jesus is God's attempt to get to us. Christianity teaches salvation comes only by God's grace through faith, not

> **Religion is a human's attempt to get to God; Jesus is God's attempt to get to us.**

human works (Ephesians 2:8–9). Now, some Christian denominations have made their own doctrinal requirements that can create the appearance of exclusivity. These requirements often do not help an individual's belief or personal relationship with God. And this relationship is what determines a person's salvation, so it's important for believers to make this distinction when sharing the gospel. We cannot earn God's love, grace, or mercy; they are freely given.

For this reason, Christianity, in its purest form, is *not* exclusive. Salvation does not depend upon your actions—it depends only upon your acceptance that Jesus has already done everything for you! You don't have to *do* anything;

> **" Salvation does not depend upon your actions—it depends only upon your acceptance that Jesus has already done everything for you! "**

you simply have to *receive someone.* You must accept the gift He has already freely offered. Throughout Scripture, you will see the word *whoever*: "Whoever calls upon the name of the Lord shall be saved" (Acts 2:21). This word makes Christianity the most *inclusive* "religion" in the world!

You may ask about people who have never heard about Jesus or who lived before Jesus came to earth. These are valid questions, and it's okay to ask them. To answer difficult questions the right way, we must filter them through the Scriptures and the One who wrote them. God's Word exhibits the character of its author. In other words, the answers come when we see evidence and understand the attributes—characteristics—of God. When you give a tribute to someone, you speak positively about things they have done or the goodness of their nature. So, to explain why Jesus is the only way, we need to understand the attributes of God.

The first attribute of God is that He is good.

> You are *good*, and do good (Psalm 119:68).
> For You, Lord, *are* good, and ready to
>   forgive,
> And abundant in mercy to all those who
>   call upon You (Psalm 86:5).

Notice the inclusivity of the psalmist's use of "all." God will forgive *all* who call upon Him. Believers must understand the goodness of God to answer questions from people who have never heard of Him. I'll use some analogies to illustrate this point.

Do you remember playing "hide and seek" as a child? God doesn't play games with us, but these two words (*hide* and *seek*) will help us remember and understand how God relates to us.

What did Adam and Eve do in the garden after they sinned? They hid. But did Adam go

looking for God? No! *God came looking for Adam.*
The Bible says,

> And they heard the sound of the Lord
> God walking in the garden in the cool
> of the day, and Adam and his wife hid
> themselves from the presence of the
> Lord God among the trees of the garden
> (Genesis 3:8).

You see, God has been seeking people from
the very beginning. And because He is seeking
people, He also reveals Himself. Jesus says this
about Himself and His Father seeking people:

> "For the Son of man has come to seek and
> to save that which was lost" (Luke 19:10).

Many other Scriptures describe the way God
reveals Himself to us:

> Then a man of God came to Eli and said
> to him, "Thus says the Lord: 'Did I not
> clearly reveal Myself to the house of

your father when they were in Egypt in
Pharaoh's house?'" (1 Samuel 2:27).

God clearly revealed Himself to Israel and all of
Egypt.

> The Lord has made known His salvation;
> His righteousness He has revealed in the
>   sight of the nations (Psalm 98:2).

The Lord made His salvation known. He
didn't hide. God is not on an undercover mission hoping people will figure out His complex
scheme. He wants everyone to be saved, so God
has made His salvation known and revealed His
righteousness to all the nations. Similar passages
are in the New Testament:

> For the wrath of God is revealed from
> heaven against all ungodliness and
> unrighteousness of men, who suppress
> the truth in unrighteousness, because
> what may be known of God is mani-
> fest in them, for God has shown *it* to

> them. For since the creation of the world
> His invisible *attributes* are clearly seen,
> being understood by the things that
> are made, *even* His eternal power and
> Godhead, so that they are without excuse
> (Romans 1:18–20).

God's attributes, including His wrath, have been made known by Him, and people have clearly seen them since the creation of the world.

We can see God's attributes clearly, not dimly. No one has an excuse because God reveals Himself to anyone who wants to know Him. Remember, God is not only a God we know by evidence—He is also a God we know by experience!

In the book of Luke, we read about a man named Cornelius who was not a follower of Jesus, but he believed in God and prayed to Him. God sent the apostle Peter to tell him about Jesus. (Remember, no one can come to the Father except through Jesus.) Since Cornelius was seeking God, God sent someone to reveal His Son to him (Acts 10).

> **Remember, God is not only a God we know by evidence—He is also a God we know by experience!**

Situations like this still happen today. In her book, *Persian Springs*, Pauline Selby tells the story of how Jesus revealed Himself to four Iranians and how each of them was saved. They had never heard the name of Jesus and had never owned or read a Bible. Still, God revealed Himself to them.

Some years ago, Ali Pektash, a Turkish Kurd, suffered from alcohol addiction. His friends persuaded him to make the Hajj, the annual pilgrimage to Islam's holy city of Mecca. They thought if Ali went to Saudi Arabia, where alcohol is banned, the Hajj might cure him.

On his way to Mecca, Ali was feeling unsatisfied and began seeking God rather than religion. He cried out to God for help. One night, Jesus appeared to Ali in a dream and touched him.

This convinced him to believe in Jesus and go back home to his family and friends.

Upon returning home, Ali's family and friends held a traditional celebration for those who had returned from the pilgrimage. At the gathering, he announced to his astonished family and friends he was now a Christian! At first, he thought he would have to leave his wife because he had become a Christian, but she immediately agreed to convert as well. For several years after his conversion, Ali didn't own a Bible or know any other Christians. But God has a way of reaching His children, and now Ali is a pastor.

Testimonies such as these have been emerging from all over the Islamic world. Jesus is coming to people in their dreams, and they are coming to faith in Him. God is revealing Himself to those who seek Him and to those who are looking for something, even though they don't know it's God they want!

Ravi Zacharias shares his testimony about an encounter he had with another man in a Muslim country. (He doesn't name the country to protect the security of the believers there.) Some friends brought the man to see Zacharias and share his testimony with him.

He said, "I was in a country that was 99% Muslim. I was in the army, and I was trained to do two things. I was trained to kill people without feeling [like ISIS does today], and I was trained to make false passports." He also said, "My brothers are in the army too, and one of them is a general." Yet every night, *for seven years*, this man had a dream about Jesus.

He told his mother about the dreams, and she told him to get out of the country. Even though he said he would not convert to Christianity, his mother said his brothers would kill him if they ever found out about the dreams. This man fled to another country where he met a Chinese businessman who was a Christian living outside of China. The businessman told the man about Jesus, and he became a Christian.

" God is truly a good God who is in the business of seeking us. "

God revealed Himself to this man. God's providence was evident. It shows God is truly a good God who is in the business of seeking us.

8

GOD IS JUST

I n the previous chapter, I wrote about "hide and seek," but God has another precept the Bible calls "seek and find." In His Sermon on the Mount, Jesus says if you ask, you will receive; if you seek, you will find; if you knock, the door will be opened (Matthew 7:7–8). He is a loving God who reveals Himself to every person, and He is a just God who is found by every person who seeks Him. It's His nature to be just. King David even tells us, "God is a just judge" (Psalm 7:11).

You're probably familiar with these words about God's goodness from the prophet Jeremiah:

> "For I know the thoughts that I think
> toward you," says the Lord, "thoughts of

> peace and not of evil, to give you a future
> and a hope" (Jeremiah 29:11).

However, you may not be quite as familiar with
the next three verses:

> "Then you will call upon Me and go and
> pray to Me, and I will listen to you. And
> you will seek Me and find *Me*, when
> you search for Me with all your heart.
> I will be found by you," says the Lord
> (Jeremiah 29:12–14).

These next two verses powerfully declare the
second attribute of God—that He is just.

> You will seek the Lord your God, and
> you will find *Him* if you seek Him with
> all your heart and with all your soul
> (Deuteronomy 4:29).

> I love those who love me,
> And those who seek me diligently will
>   find me (Proverbs 8:17).

Read this passage from the sermon the apostle Paul preaches in Athens:

> And He has made from one blood every
> nation of men to dwell on all the face
> of the earth, and has determined their
> preappointed times and the boundaries
> of their dwellings, so that they should
> seek the Lord, in the hope that they
> might grope for [seek] Him and find Him,
> though He is not far from each one of us
> (Acts 17:26–27).

God would not be a just God if He sent someone to hell who never had a chance to believe. But I *know* God is a just God, and every single person who seeks Him will find Him. Even so, there may be times when you have questions, such as "How could Jesus be the only way?" or "What happens to people who have never heard?" When you have questions, go back to the Bible and find passages where God says if we seek Him, we'll find Him. He will reveal Himself to everyone!

> **You don't have to know everything to seek God with all you have. If you search for Him with *all your heart*, you will find Him.**

You don't have to know everything to seek God with all you have. If you search for Him with *all your heart*, you will find Him. As I noted earlier, Paul says, "His *invisible* attributes are clearly seen … they are without excuse" (Romans 1:20).

I love this story illustrating the amazing way God shows His goodness and justice:

More than 130 years ago, in a small Liberian village in West Africa, there was a young son of a Kru tribal chieftain named Prince Kaboo. While still a child, a neighboring clan defeated his people and demanded Kaboo's father pay a hefty ransom for his son's return.

The conquering chief subjected Kaboo to terrible treatment and cruel labor. During one of many intense whippings, he saw a bright light and heard a voice from heaven telling him to flee. The rope that was binding him fell to the ground; he gathered his strength and ran into the jungle.

Traveling at night and hiding in the hollow of trees by day, Kaboo navigated blindly through a jungle dominated by jungle law. Eventually he arrived at Monrovia, the capital of Liberia and the one civilized city with thousands of Liberians under governmental law. There, a young boy invited Kaboo to church, where Miss Knolls, a missionary and graduate of Taylor University (then known as Fort Wayne College), spoke on the conversion of the apostle Paul. Kaboo immediately saw similarities between his story and Paul's. Shortly afterward, he accepted Christ as his Savior and was baptized under the name of Samuel Morris, in honor of the missionary's benefactor.

Samuel spent the next two years painting houses in Monrovia. He became a zealous member of the Christian community and displayed a fervent desire to learn about the Holy Spirit. He was encouraged to travel to America and seek instruction from Stephen Merritt, former secretary to Bishop William Taylor. With no money or means of transportation, Samuel began his journey on foot.

Sleeping on the beach at the Robertsport harbor, he waited for several days before finding passage on a ship in exchange for work. The journey was difficult, and he was often beaten and assigned the most difficult tasks. However, by the time the ship docked in New York in September 1891, the captain and most of the crew had accepted Jesus because of Samuel's witness.

Once he arrived in America, Stephen Merritt warmly received Samuel. He contacted Thaddeus Reade, then president of Taylor University, and requested to enroll him at the school. Due to the university's financial debt, Reade started a fund for Samuel, which would later be known as the "Faith Fund."

In December 1891, Samuel arrived on Taylor University's campus (then in Fort Wayne,

Indiana). When asked by Reade which room he wanted, he replied, "If there is a room nobody wants, give it to me." Samuel's faith had such a profound impact on the Fort Wayne community that he was frequently invited to speak at local churches. At night, he could be heard in his room praying, which he simply called "talking to my Father."

President Reade once said, "Samuel Morris was a divinely sent messenger of God to Taylor University. He thought he was coming here to prepare himself for his mission to his people, but his coming was to prepare Taylor University for her mission to the whole world. All who met him were impressed with his sublime, yet simple faith in God."

On May 12, 1893, Samuel Morris died at the age of 20 after contracting a severe cold. His death inspired his fellow students to serve as missionaries to Africa on his behalf, fulfilling his dream of one day returning to minister to his own people.[1]

Today, if you go to Taylor University, there is a dormitory called Samuel Morris Hall. The university constructed this building with the proceeds from the sales of a biography about this young man's life, entitled *Angel in Ebony*.

God is good, and He is just, and when a young African man cried out to Him, God revealed Himself and brought him to Christ.

9

GOD IS LOVE

The third attribute of God is love. His goodness and justice are demonstrations of His love for us. C. S. Lewis brilliantly illustrates this point:

> There are two types of people in the world, the person who bows his knee to God and says "Your will be done," and the person who does not bow his knee to God, and God says, "All right, then your will be done." All that are in Hell, choose it. Without that self-choice there could be no Hell. No soul that seriously and constantly desires joy will ever miss it. Those who seek find. Those who knock it is opened.[1]

This statement is as fair as it can be. God gives people free will. He reveals Himself to every person, and He gives all people the ability to choose where they are going to spend eternity. They can choose whether to love Him or not. No person can say, "God is rejecting me." However, God can truthfully say to a person, "You are rejecting Me." This choice grows out of God's great love for us.

John 3:16, one of the most well-known verses in the Bible, talks about His love for us:

> For God so loved the world that he gave
> his only begotten Son, that whoever
> believes in Him should not perish but
> have everlasting life.

In order to illustrate the extraordinary nature of God's love, I'll use a linguistic example. When we use words, we use them in one of three ways: univocally, equivocally, and analogically.

1. The prefix *uni-* in univocally means one or the same. If you are speaking univocally, you are using the word in only one way, though it could be used differently.
2. Equivocally means you are using a word with different meanings. You might use the same word but mean it in a different way.
3. If you use a word analogically, it means you are using a word and it has a higher or deeper meaning than the way you are using it.

If I am speaking about my wife, Debbie, I use the word *love* univocally and say, "I love you, and Debbie loves you." You can see the meaning of the word *love* in this sentence is applied the same way. If I use the same word equivocally, however, I could say, "I love you, and I love Debbie." Clearly, I don't love you in the same way and with the same meaning as I love Debbie.

But when we speak of God, we can only speak analogically. Here's an example of the analogical meaning of the word "good" as it applies to God: If you were to ask me, "Pastor Robert, are you a good golfer?" I would say, "I'm a good golfer—not great but good." Now, suppose you're on a plane and sit down next to a man you don't know and start a conversation. The man introduces himself and says, "I'm Phil Mickelson." You haven't heard of him before, but you find out he plays golf for a living. You ask him, "Are you a good golfer?" And he responds, "Yes, I would say I'm a good golfer."

Even though Phil and I used the same word ("good"), it would be a *huge* mistake if you said to Phil, "Well, you ought to play golf with Pastor Robert because he's a good golfer too." It's the same word but with two vastly different meanings. This is an example of two entirely different types of good.

God's goodness is so much better than our goodness, His justice is so much higher than our justice, and His love is so much deeper than our love that the only way we can describe it is analogically. It's difficult to express how much God loves you in simple terms, so I'm going to use an analogy.

If I say, "I love you," and you refuse my love, I hurt because I've lost something. When God says He loves you, and you refuse His love, He hurts because *you've* lost something. *God's love is a completely unselfish love.*

> **" God's love is a completely unselfish love. "**

It's recorded two times in the Bible that Jesus wept. The first time was after the death of Lazarus (John 11:35). Jesus did not weep because *He* had lost something; He knew He was going to raise Lazarus from the dead. He wept when He saw the grief of Mary and Martha, the sisters of Lazarus. Jesus wept because *they* had lost something.

The second time Jesus wept was when He entered the city of Jerusalem. He wept then because He knew Jerusalem had lost something.

He knew the present generation was going to reject Him as the Messiah and the Temple would be destroyed. Both of these were great losses to the people.

God is still offering His love to you today. He gives you the choice to receive it, but if you reject it, you'll lose everything. *Everything.*

> 66 **God is still offering His love to you today. He gives you the choice to receive it, but if you reject it, you'll lose everything.** *Everything.* 99

Don't get distracted by the fact there is *only one way*. Rejoice in knowing there is *a way* and be excited God has revealed this way to you in Jesus Christ. The evidence from the Bible and the experiences of millions of people testify to Jesus as the only way. You have a free will—you can accept His love, or you can reject it. Again, no person can truthfully say to God, "You are rejecting me." But God can truthfully say to a person, "You are rejecting Me."

THIS IS HOW I KNOW JESUS IS THE ONLY WAY:

1. The evidence:

- The finite world exists; therefore, an infinite God had to cause it.
- The Bible has been proven to be miraculously accurate and true.
- The Bible, being accurate and true, records the true events of Jesus' miraculous and divine life.
- In the accurate and true New Testament, Jesus says, "I am the way, the truth, and the life. No one comes to the Father except through Me" (John 14:6). The evidence of Jesus' miraculous life and the evidence of the Bible's miraculous reliability prove the trustworthiness of Jesus' words.

2. I know Jesus by the attributes of God:

- God is *good*. His goodness is so much better than our goodness. We can see His goodness in His providence and the work of His people. He has revealed Himself in many ways.
- God is *just*. His justice is so much higher than our justice. He makes salvation freely available to anyone who will seek Him.
- God is *love*. His love is so much deeper than our love. He will not reject you. He offers His love and its greatest rewards because He does not want you to miss the joys of heaven.

FOR DISCUSSION & PERSONAL REFLECTION

Focus

Christianity is the most inclusive religion in the world. The Lord will reveal Himself to anyone who seeks Him, and He gives every person the choice to receive Him. The Lord is a good, just, and loving God who provided the way for us to be saved through His Son, Jesus Christ.

Key Scriptures

Jesus said to him, "I am the way, the truth, and the life. No one comes to the Father except through Me" (John 14:6).

"There is no other name under heaven
given among men by which we must be
saved" (Acts 4:12).

Review

God Is Good

Psalm 98:2; 119:68; Romans 1:19–20

The Bible says God is always ready to forgive.
He doesn't hide from us or exclude anyone. He
reveals Himself to every person who reaches out
to Him. Anyone in the world can come to Him.

God Is Just

Psalm 7:11; Jeremiah 29:11–14; Acts 17:25–27

Not only does God reveal Himself to everyone who seeks Him, He is also *found* by all who
seek Him diligently—with their whole heart.
The Bible says if you seek Him, you *will* find
Him. To give a person the dignity of freedom to
choose and then violate this freedom would not
be fair. God is just and fair and cannot lie.

God Is Love

John 3:16

Christianity is inclusive, not exclusive. The Bible says *whoever seeks Him* will find Him. Not just some or a few, but any person who seeks the Lord will find Him. A person can never say God is rejecting him, but unfortunately, God can say a person is rejecting Him. God loved us enough to send His Son to die for us. It's our choice to choose Jesus as our Lord and Savior.

Discussion or Personal Reflection

1. How did the Lord reveal Himself to you when you first began seeking Him? How has He revealed Himself to you in the last week?

2. What does it mean to you to know if you seek the Lord you *will* find Him? How can you pray for your unbelieving friends to find the Lord?

3. Read Proverbs 8:17. Notice the word "diligently." Describe how a person can

diligently seek the Lord. How does this concept apply to your life?

4. What are some obstacles that may prevent a person from believing God truly and completely loves them? What is the outcome of living with the belief God could not love them?

5. How do you know God loves you? How would you explain God's love to someone who doesn't believe in God?

Take It with You

- Christianity is inclusive, not exclusive.
- God has promised to reveal Himself to any person who seeks Him, and He promises they will find Him when they seek Him.
- God loves us so much that He sent His Son, Jesus, to die for our sins.
- God gives us the free will to decide whom we will serve, and we all have the choice to submit our will to Jesus Christ.

- Pray for those who do not know Jesus as their Savior to reach out to Him in some way.

Prayer

Lord, thank You for Your goodness. And thank You for giving mercy and grace to all who call on Your name. Lord, help those who don't know You to see You as good, just, and loving. I ask for You to reveal Yourself to my friends and family who have not accepted You. Make Yourself known to them. In Jesus' name, Amen.

CONCLUSION

The next time you are questioning the existence of God, the authority of the Bible, or Jesus as Savior, remember the evidence is all around you. Seek God in the physical world, whether it is the beauty of a sunrise or a single flower. Seek Him in prayer and in the spiritual realm. Prepare to experience the power and providence of God, if you seek Him diligently. Go to God's Word and listen for His voice. His Holy Spirit will lead you where you need to go. You will find Him. He will find you. And remember, there are people praying for you, even at this very moment.

> **His Holy Spirit will lead you where you need to go.**

For this reason we also, since the day we heard it, do not cease to pray for you, and to ask that you may be filled with the knowledge of His will in all wisdom and spiritual understanding; that you may walk worthy of the Lord, fully pleasing *Him,* being fruitful in every good work and increasing in the knowledge of God; strengthened with all might, according to His glorious power, for all patience and longsuffering with joy; giving thanks to the Father who has qualified us to be partakers of the inheritance of the saints in the light (Colossians 1:9–12).

ABOUT THE AUTHOR

Robert Morris is the founding senior pastor of Gateway Church, a multi-campus church in the Dallas/ Fort Worth Metroplex. Since it began in 2000, the church has grown to more than 39,000 active members. His daily and weekly television program is aired in over 190 countries, and his radio program, *Worship & the Word with Pastor Robert Morris,* is featured on radio stations across America. He serves as chancellor of The King's University and has written 15 books. These include *The God I Never Knew, Truly Free, Frequency,* and the bestseller *The Blessed Life.* Robert and his wife, Debbie, have been married 38 years and are blessed with one married daughter, two married sons, and nine grandchildren.

NOTES

Chapter 1: A Correct Worldview

1. The following list outlines the seven major worldviews: *Theism*: One God created the universe and is involved in it today. *Atheism:* There is no God. Instead, there is a natural inner working of the universe. *Pantheism*: God is all that exists, and all that exists is God. God is all. *Panentheism*: God is *in* all. *Polytheism*: There is not one God but many gods. *Deism*: There is a Creator God, but this God is totally uninvolved in this world. Deism follows atheism's belief in the natural inner workings of the universe. *Finite Godism*: God is limited, not infinite, which explains an imperfect world. Example: The theory of evolution is a view that often stems from the major worldviews of atheism and deism. See Norman Geisler, *Systematic Theology Introduction Bible Vol. 1* (Minneapolis: Bethany House, 2002), 19–21; Matt Slick, "An Introduction to Apologetics," CARM, accessed September 11, 2016, https://carm.org/what-is-atheism.

2. Ravi Zacharias, "How do you know that Christianity is

the one true worldview?" YouTube, April 02, 2012, accessed March 04, 2018, https://www.youtube.com /watch?v=nWY-6xBA0Pk.

3. For example, see *Can Man Live without God* (Dallas: W Publishing Group, 1994); *Jesus Among Other Gods: The Absolute Claims of the Christian Message* (Nashville: Thomas Nelson, 2000); and Ravi K. Zacharias and Norman L. Geisler*, Who Made God?: And Answers to Over 100 Other Tough Questions of Faith* (Grand Rapids: Zondervan, 2003).

4. John N. Clayton, "Why I Left Atheism," Does God Exist? last modified October 23, 2012, accessed March 01, 2018, http://www.doesgodexist.org/AboutClayton/PastLife.html.

5. Charles Darwin, *On the Origin of Species: By Means of Natural Selection* (London: John Murray, 1859).

6. See Thomas Aquinas, *Summa Theologica* (Westminster, MD: Christian Classics, 1981), 10. Aquinas is one of the greatest theologians in church history. He authored numerous books on philosophy and theology and is known for his teaching on the five proofs. Aquinas' second proof, titled *Arguments for Efficient Cause*, points to the fact that the entire universe we live in, and everything in it, is finite. In the finite realm, no example has ever existed of something that caused itself to exist. The only way a finite universe can exist is if there is an original cause beyond the finite world. Aquinas wrote, "Therefore, it is necessary to admit a first efficient cause, to which the name 'God' is given".

7. Ravi Zacharias, "Why are you so afraid of subjective moral reasoning?" YouTube, February 15, 2014, accessed

March 04, 2018, https://www.youtube.com /watch?v=0218GkAGbnU.

8. See Aquinas, *Summa Theologica*, 10. Aquinas also spoke of objective morality and its source. His fourth proof for the existence of God was *Argument From the Gradation of Being*, in which he showed how there are quantities and qualities found in things that originate from the original. Humans come from God; therefore, they have attributes and qualities resembling Him. Human beings possess a moral compass because God is the great moral compass; humans are an extension of the original. Numerous moral absolutes transcend culture, making it difficult for someone to argue that they exist by chance. Aquinas concluded, "Therefore, something must exist that is to all beings the cause of their being, goodness, and every other perfection; and this being is God."

Chapter 2: The Foolishness of Atheism

1. F.W.H. Petrie, ed., *Journal of the Transaction of the Victoria Institute, or Philosophical Society of Great Britain Vol. XXXI* (London: The Institute, 1899), 267

2. See Norman L. Geisler, *Teacher's Guide: Twelve Points That Show Christianity Is True* (Indian Trail, NC: Norm Geisler International Ministries, 2016), 71. Geisler outlines further evidence for God's existence; it is not a scientific impossibility. Biblical scholars often refer to the Cosmological Argument. The Cosmological Argument looks backwards to the beginning of time and states: Whatever had a beginning,

had a Beginner (Cause). The universe had a beginning. Therefore, the universe had a Beginner (Cause). This argument again solidifies the fact that the finite does not exist without the infinite, and it exposes the ridiculous notion of atheism. The entire existence of our universe operates on the scientific basis that something cannot come to exist out of nothing, but everything in existence was caused by something that was here before it was. Atheists at the very least must admit that they do not possess all knowledge. It would be silly to claim otherwise. Atheists must also admit that this world didn't just appear out of nothing. Something (God) caused it to exist.

Chapter 4: The Bible Is Amazing

1. Josh McDowell and Clay Jones, "The Bibliographical Test," Josh McDowell Ministry, last modified August 13, 14, accessed September 10, 2016, http://www.josh.org/wp -content/uploads/Bibliographical-Test-Update-08.13.14.pdf.
2. Norman Geisler, *Systematic Theology Introduction Bible Vol. 1* (Minneapolis: Bethany House, 2002), 463.
3. Bruce M. Metzger, *The Text of the New Testament* (New York and Oxford: Oxford University Press, 1968), 34.
4. Peter W. Stoner, *Science Speaks, Scientific Proof of the Accuracy of Prophecy and the Bible*, Online Edition revised by Donald W. Stoner (Chicago: Moody Press, 2005), chap. 3, http://science speaks.dstoner.net/Christ_of_Prophecy.html#c9.
5. Peter W. Stoner, *Science Speaks, Scientific Proof of the Accuracy*

of Prophecy and the Bible, Foreword, http://sciencespeaks
.dstoner.net/index.html#c2.

6. Peter W. Stoner, *Science Speaks, Scientific Proof of the Accuracy
of Prophecy and the Bible*, chap. 3.

Part Two Study Guide

1. Josh McDowell, *The New Evidence That Demands a
Verdict: Evidence I & II Fully Updated in One Volume to Answer
the Questions Challenging Christians in the 21st Century* (San
Bernardino, CA: Here's Life Publishers, 1999).

Chapter 8: God is Just

1. Adapted from "The Samuel Morris Story," Taylor
University, accessed September 06, 2016, http://www.taylor
.edu/about/heritage/samuel-morris/the-samuel-morris-story
.shtml.

Chapter 9: God Is Love

1. C.S. Lewis, *The Great Divorce* (United Kingdom: Geoffrey
Bles, 1945).